the Worship
PIANO METHOD
LEVEL 2

By Wendy Stevens and Teresa Ledford

Page numbers of specific pieces are shown on the CD Track List.

ISBN 978-1-61774-041-1

HAL•LEONARD®
CORPORATION

7777 W. BLUEMOUND RD. P.O. BOX 13819 MILWAUKEE, WI 53213

In Australia Contact:
Hal Leonard Australia Pty. Ltd.
4 Lentara Court
Cheltenham, 3192 Victoria, Australia
Email: ausadmin@halleonard.com.au

Visit Hal Leonard Online at
www.halleonard.com

LEVEL 1 REVIEW

RHYTHM

✏️ Write the correct number of beats for each note or rest.

Clap the following rhythms. Be sure to count each beat!

Beginning notes in an incomplete measure are called _____ notes.

NOTES

✏️ 1. Write the correct letter name of each note in the blanks.

2. Draw the notes above or below that share the same letter name.

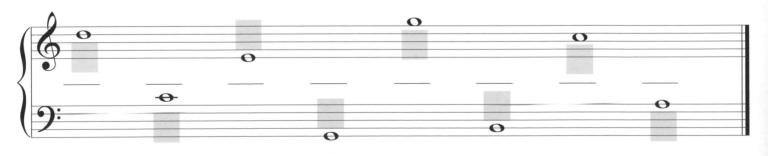

SYMBOLS

 Match each symbol with its correct term and meaning.

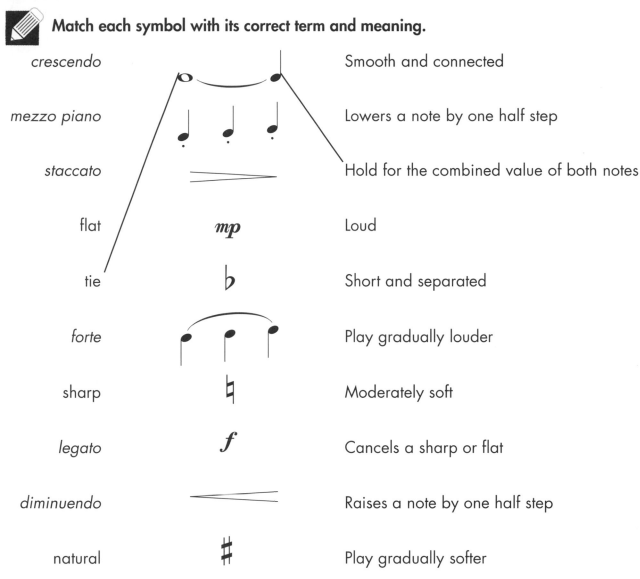

crescendo   Smooth and connected

mezzo piano   Lowers a note by one half step

staccato   Hold for the combined value of both notes

flat   Loud

tie   Short and separated

forte   Play gradually louder

sharp   Moderately soft

legato   Cancels a sharp or flat

diminuendo   Raises a note by one half step

natural   Play gradually softer

INTERVALS

 Write the correct name of each interval in the blanks.

Example:

3rd

As you begin Level 2, keep this Bible verse in mind:

"Sing to Him a new song; play skillfully with a shout of joy."
– Psalm 33:3, NASB®

"'…I am the Light of the world;
he who follows Me will not walk in the darkness,
but will have the Light of life.'"
– John 8:12, NASB

You're the Light

By Wendy Stevens

TRACKS 1-2

With energy ♩ = 160

You're the Light, You're the Light, You're the Light in the dark-ness. You shine

bright in the night, You are bright-er than the day. We o-

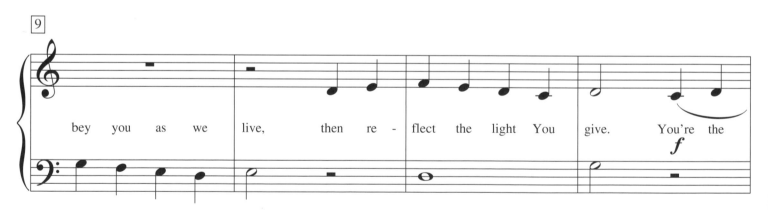

bey you as we live, then re-flect the light You give. You're the

Light, You're the Light, You're the Light of the world.

Chords

A **chord** is a group of notes that are played together. A **triad** is a special three-note chord. You can build a triad with three notes that are skips from each other. This is called a **root position** triad.

The bottom note names the chord and is called the root. The middle note is called the 3rd and the top note is called the 5th.

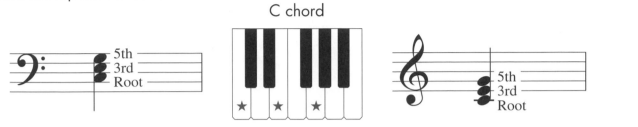

 Circle all the C chords in this piece.

God Is So Good

TRACKS 3-4

Traditional
Arranged by Teresa Ledford

Additional verses:

I love Him so…
I praise His name…

 Write your own verse!

_____

"The Lord is good to those who hope in Him, to those who seek Him."

– *Lamentations 3:25, NCV®*

5

When the Saints Go Marching In

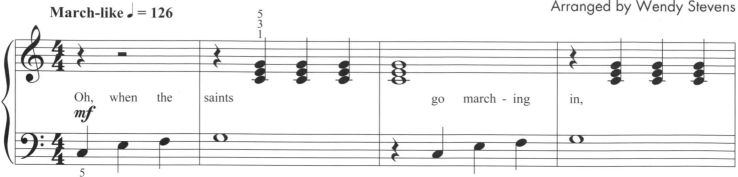

TRACKS 5-6

Words by Katherine E. Purvis
Music by James M. Black
Arranged by Wendy Stevens

March-like ♩ = 126

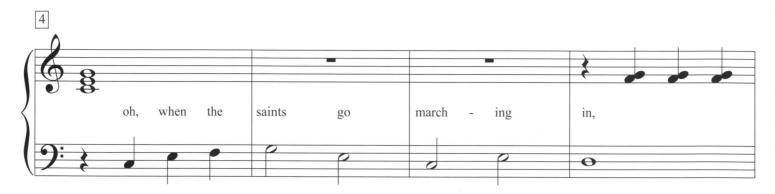

Oh, when the saints go march - ing in,

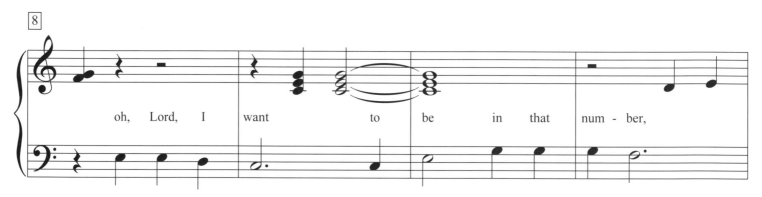

oh, when the saints go march - ing in,

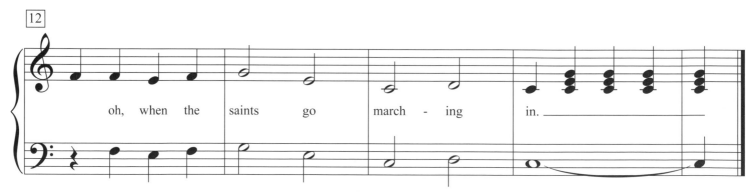

oh, Lord, I want to be in that num - ber,

oh, when the saints go march - ing in.

I Am a C-H-R-I-S-T-I-A-N

Traditional
Arranged by Teresa Ledford

TRACKS 7-8

F chord

"...God has given us eternal life, and this life is in His Son."
– 1 John 5:11, NASB

G chord

These are the same notes.

Circle all the G chords in this piece.

TRACKS 9-10

It's Me, O Lord

Traditional Spiritual
Arranged by Teresa Ledford

Quickly ♩ = 176

It's me, it's me, it's me, O

Lord, stand - in' in the need of

1. prayer. It's

2. prayer.

DRAWING CHORDS

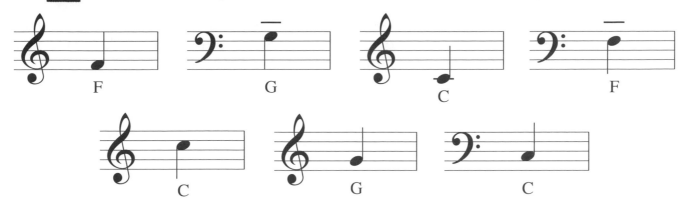

Draw the following chords on the staff. The roots are drawn for you.

F   G   C   F

C   G   C

IDENTIFYING CHORDS

To create your stained glass window:

Color the C chords red.

Color the F chords green.

Color the G chords blue.

Color the cross yellow.

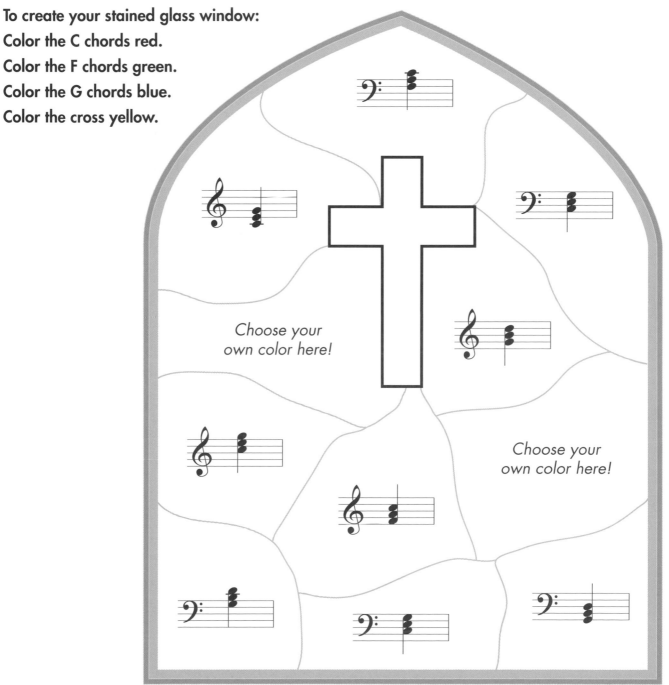

Choose your own color here!

Choose your own color here!

Lead Sheets
CHORD SYMBOLS

A lead sheet is a piece of music that shows the melody with chord symbols above it. When playing with other instruments, pianists often have to locate and play these chords with their left hand without seeing them on the staff.

 Draw the left-hand chords under the melody of "O Worship the King." (The first line has been done for you.) Use the C, F and G chords in these positions:

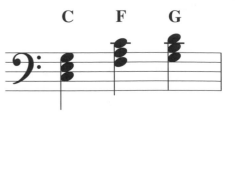

 While your teacher plays this melody, play the chords you have written with your left hand.

O Worship the King

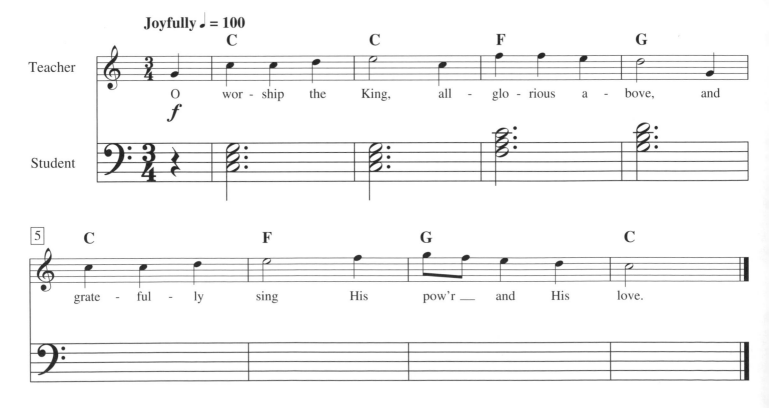

TRACKS 11-12

Words by Robert Grant
Music attributed to Johann Michael Haydn

TRACKS 13-14

While your teacher plays this melody, play the chords with your left hand. (Use whole notes.)

What a Friend We Have in Jesus

Words by Joseph M. Scriven
Music by Charles C. Converse

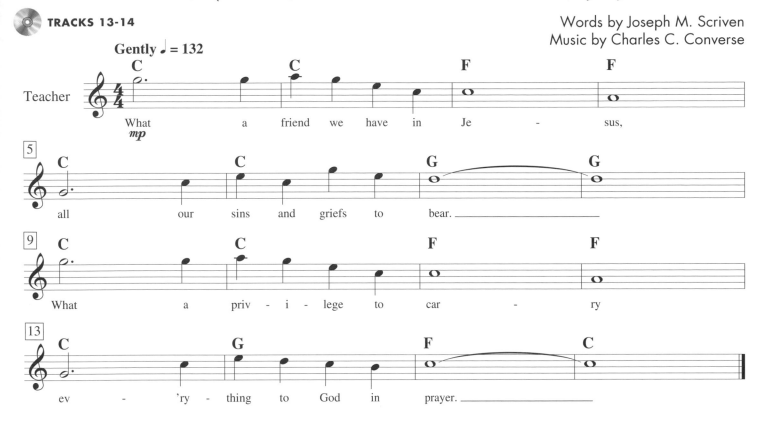

Gently ♩ = 132

Teacher

What a friend we have in Je - sus,

5 all our sins and griefs to bear.

9 What a priv - i - lege to car - ry

13 ev - 'ry - thing to God in prayer.

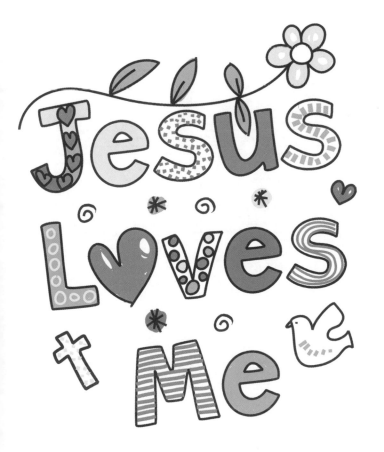

Jesus Loves Me

"Give all your worries to Him, because He cares about you."
– I Peter 5:7, NCV

8va - - - ⌐, **Octave**

When you see an *8va* sign above a group of notes, play those notes one **octave** higher. An octave is the distance from one note to the next higher or lower note with the same letter name.

In measures 1-3, what chord is broken into its individual notes? _____

Harps of Gold

TRACKS 15-16

By Wendy Stevens

Hold down the damper pedal throughout this piece.

12

Major and Minor Chords

A Major chord contains four half steps between the root and the 3rd.

Remember, a half step is the distance between one note and the very next higher or lower note (white or black).

A minor chord contains three half steps between the root and the 3rd.

> Begin counting half steps *after* the starting note.

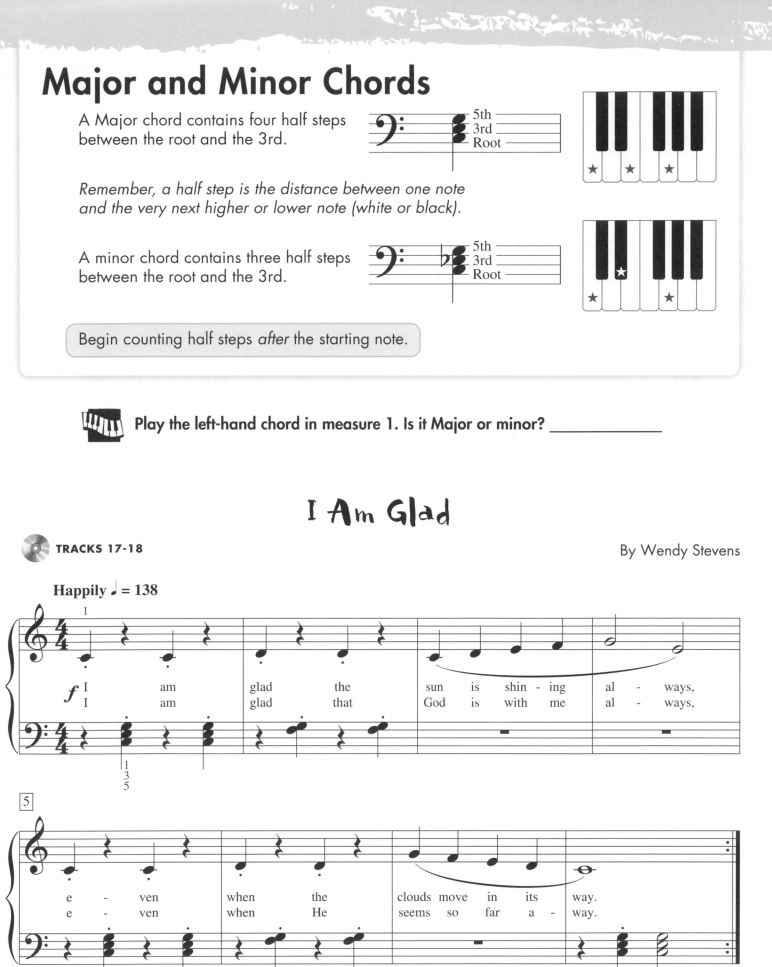

Play the left-hand chord in measure 1. Is it Major or minor? _____

I Am Glad

TRACKS 17-18

By Wendy Stevens

Happily ♩ = 138

I am glad the sun is shin - ing al - ways,
I am glad that God is with me al - ways,

e - ven when the clouds move in its way.
e - ven when He seems so far a - way.

13

Play the left-hand chord in measure 1. Is it Major or minor? _____

God Is Near

TRACKS 19-20

By Wendy Stevens

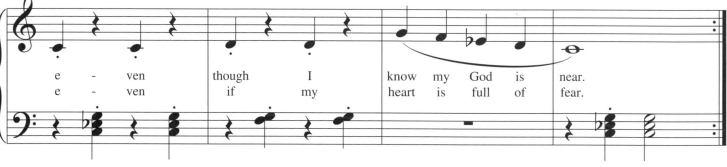

Mysteriously ♩ = 138

mp

I am scared when storms be - gin to gath - er,
I will trust in God be - cause He loves me,

5

e - ven though I know my God is near.
e - ven if my heart is full of fear.

Play the left-hand chord in measure 1. Is it Major or minor? _____

While I Sleep

TRACKS 21-22

By Wendy Stevens

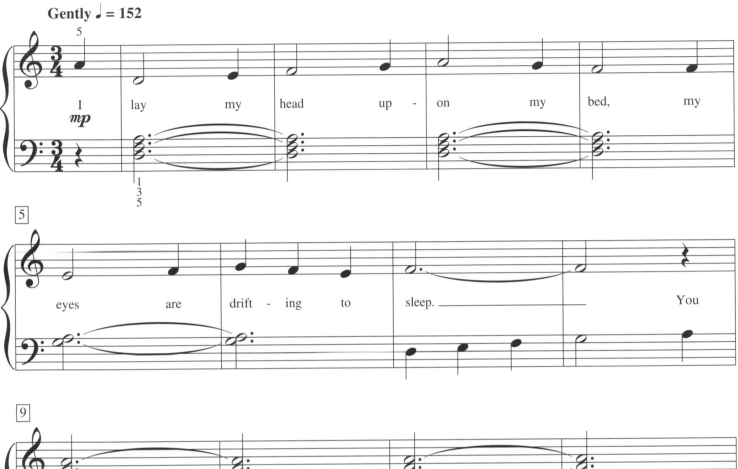

Gently ♩ = 152

I lay my head up - on my bed, my

eyes are drift - ing to sleep. _____ You

safe - ly keep me while I sleep; I

wake, for You will sus - tain me. _____

rit.

15

"X" MARKS THE CHORD

 Build the following Major and minor chords by drawing an "X" where the 3rd of the chord should be.

Remember:

A Major chord contains four half steps between the root and the 3rd.

A minor chord contains three half steps between the root and the 3rd.

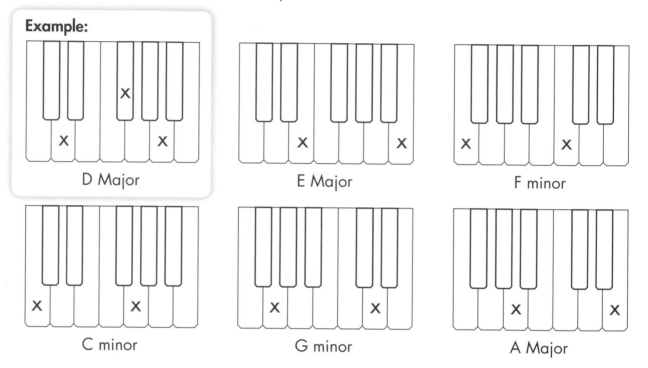

 Play these chords and label them as Major or minor, based on how they sound. Check your answers by counting the half steps. (Include the root letter name.)

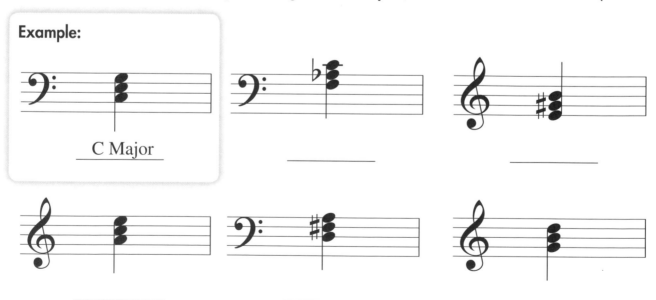

You Pick Me Up

TRACKS 23-24

By Wendy Stevens

With a groove ♩ = 168

mp   I run to You,   You make me new,

You pick me up   when I have fall - en.
You pick me up, *f*

You pick me up when I have fall - en.

Eighth Notes

♪♪ = ♩ Two eighth notes equal one quarter note.

Clap this rhythm twice, counting the first time and saying the words the second time.

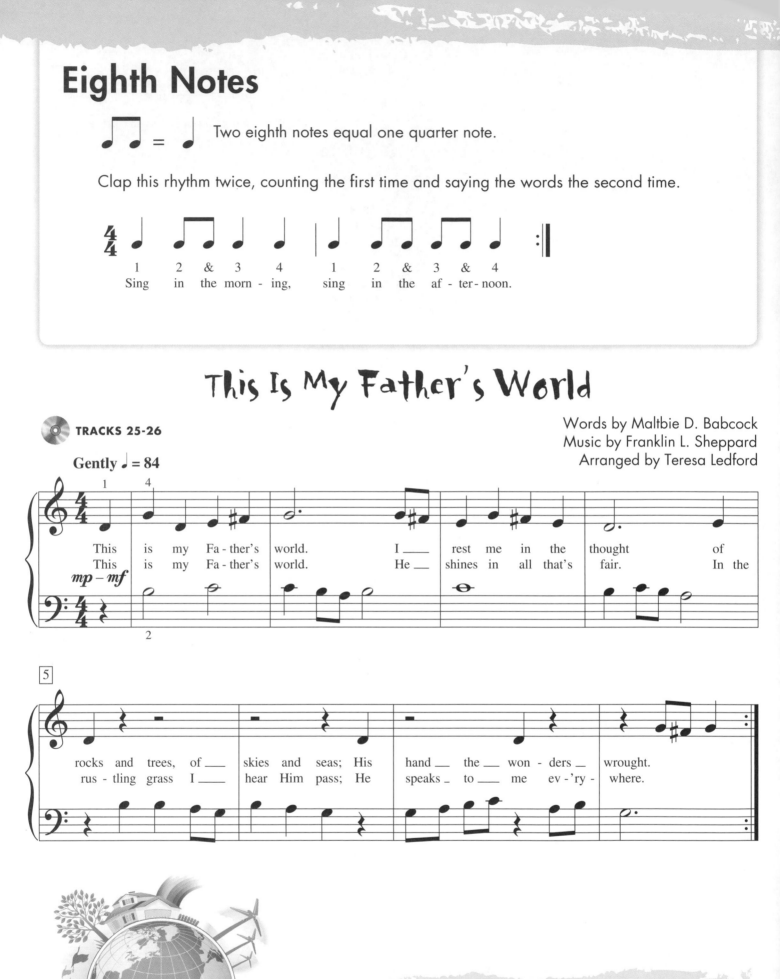

1	2	&	3	4	1	2	&	3	&	4
Sing	in	the	morn-	ing,	sing	in	the	af-	ter-	noon.

This Is My Father's World

TRACKS 25-26

Words by Maltbie D. Babcock
Music by Franklin L. Sheppard
Arranged by Teresa Ledford

Gently ♩ = 84

This is my Fa-ther's world. I ___ rest me in the thought of
This is my Fa-ther's world. He ___ shines in all that's fair. In the

mp – mf

rocks and trees, of ___ skies and seas; His hand ___ the ___ won-ders ___ wrought.
rus-tling grass I ___ hear Him pass; He speaks ___ to ___ me ev-'ry- where.

"The God who made the whole world and everything in it is the Lord of the land and the sky."

– Acts 17:24, NCV

18

I Sing the Mighty Power of God

Words by Isaac Watts
Traditional English Melody
Arranged by Teresa Ledford

TRACKS 27-28

Tags

In Level 1, you learned how to create a tag by repeating and/or stretching out the last part of a song.

Experiment with ways to add a tag to this hymn. Here are some suggestions:

- Repeat the last four measures, including the pickup beat before measure 13.
- Repeat the last two measures as written, including the pickup beat before measure 15.
- Repeat the last two measures, but double the note values.

EIGHTH NOTE ACTIVITIES

1. Circle the eighth notes that are drawn correctly.
2. Draw an "X" through the eighth notes that are not drawn correctly.

1. Follow the directions under each measure.
2. Clap the rhythm while counting out loud.

Draw one whole note.   Draw two half notes.

Draw four quarter notes.   Draw eight eighth notes (four pairs).

Notice that each measure contains notes that are twice as fast as the previous measure.

1. Clap and count the following rhythms.

Suggested Lyrics:
We will sing and praise.
Praise Him in the morning.
Mighty God, King of kings.

2. Write lyrics under each rhythm. Suggestions have been provided above, but you may write your own lyrics as well.

1. Write the beats under this rhythm. On which beat do the pickup notes start? ____

2. Clap the rhythm several times. Watch out for the tie!

All Day Long

TRACKS 29-30

Traditional Spiritual
Arranged by Teresa Ledford

Steadily ♩ = 66

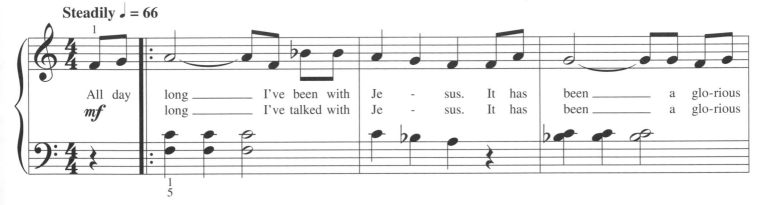

All day / long _____ I've been with / long _____ I've talked with Je - sus. It has been _____ a glo-rious

mf

day. I've just / day. It has moved _____ up one step / moved _____ me one step high - er, and I'm / high - er on my

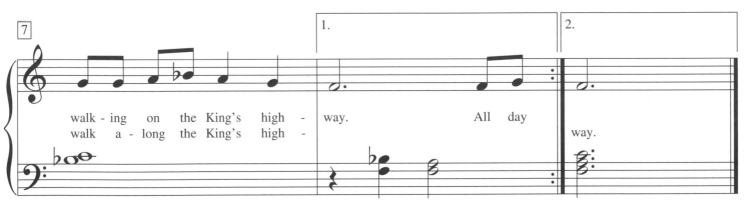

walk - ing on the King's high - / walk a - long the King's high - way. All day / way.

"How I love Your teachings!
I think about them all day long."
– Psalm 119:97, NCV

Key Signatures

Instead of writing in all the accidentals (sharps, flats and naturals), composers use key signatures to indicate which notes are always sharp or flat in a piece of music.

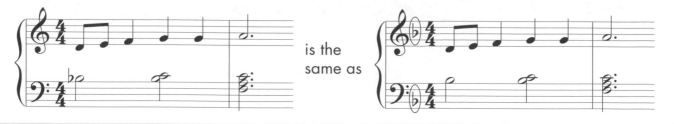

is the same as

 In the examples below, circle all the notes that are made flat or sharp by the key signature.

Play the following familiar excerpts, paying careful attention to the key signature.

This is the key of C Major. It has no sharps or flats.

This is the key of G Major. It has one sharp. Circle all the F♯ notes.

This is the key of F Major. It has one flat. Circle all the B♭ notes.

The following hymn is shown in two different keys. Play both to hear the difference.

Nothing But the Blood

TRACKS 31-32

Words and Music by
Robert Lowry
Arranged by Wendy Stevens

This version is in the key of C Major.

Confidently ♩ = 92

What can wash a - way my sin? Noth-ing but the blood of Je - sus.

What can make me whole _ a - gain? Noth-ing but the blood of Je - sus.

Nothing But the Blood

TRACKS 33-34

Words and Music by
Robert Lowry
Arranged by Wendy Stevens

This version is in the key of F Major. Circle all the B♭ notes.

Confidently ♩ = 92

What can wash a - way my sin? Noth-ing but the blood of Je - sus.

What can make me whole _ a - gain? Noth-ing but the blood of Je - sus.

Transposing

Transposing means moving a piece of music to a different key.

Many times, pianists are asked to transpose a piece of music, especially when the original music contains notes that are too high or too low for the singers.

When transposing, it is best to look at the **intervals** (the distance between the notes) rather than the notes themselves.

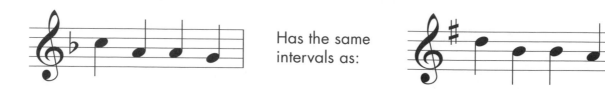

Has the same intervals as:

You are the pianist for three soloists. Each soloist wants their music transposed to a new key. Draw a line to the correct transposition of the song that each vocalist is singing.

"I'd like this transposed down a whole step."

(A whole step equals two half steps.)

"I'd like this transposed up a whole step."

"I'd like this transposed down to the key of C."

Transpose this G Major piece down one whole step to F Major.
Write the correct notes in the 2nd example.

All Hail the Power of Jesus' Name
(G Major)

Words by Edward Perronet
Music by Oliver Holden

Majestically ♩ = 108

All hail the pow'r of Je - sus' name! Let an - gels pros - trate fall.

All Hail the Power of Jesus' Name
(F Major)

Words by Edward Perronet
Music by Oliver Holden

Majestically ♩ = 108

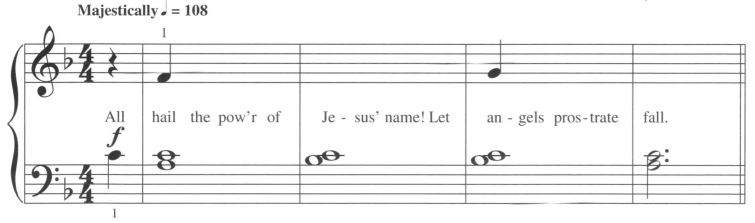

All hail the pow'r of Je - sus' name! Let an - gels pros - trate fall.

 Play the new F Major version to make sure the melody matches the G Major example.

My Shepherd

Words by Isaac Watts
Paraphrased from Psalm 23
Traditional English Melody
Arranged by Teresa Ledford

Label the chords "Major" or "minor" in the blanks below.

Moderately fast ♩ = 92

My __ Shep - herd will sup - ply my need; Je - ho - vah is __ His

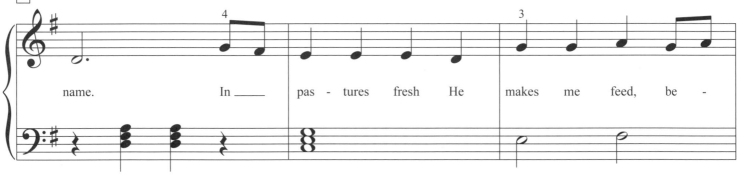

name. In _____ pas - tures fresh He makes me feed, be -

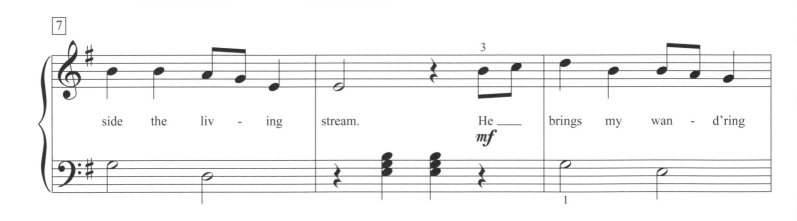

side the liv - ing stream. He _____ brings my wan - d'ring

spir - it back   when I for - sake His   ways,   and ___

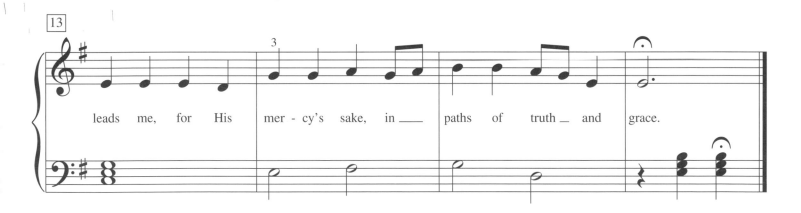

leads me, for His   mer - cy's sake, in ___ paths of truth ___ and   grace.

The ⌢ symbol in measure 16 is called a **fermata**. It tells you to hold the notes longer than their normal value. Fermatas are often found over the final notes of a piece.

D.C. al Fine

D.C. al Fine means to go back to the beginning of the piece, and play until the **Fine**.
D.C. stands for *da capo* (or "the cap"). Fine means "the end."

1. Play this piece as written.

2. Transpose the first two lines up to the key of G Major (don't play the second page).

In the Stillness

 TRACKS 37-38

By Wendy Stevens

Peacefully ♩ = 112

2nd time both hands 8va

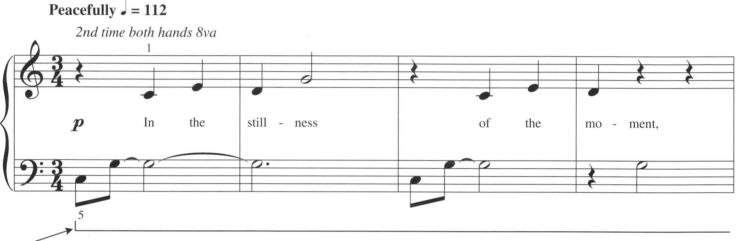

Hold down the damper pedal
until the end of measure 8.

9 *mp* You have said You'll be with me, see - ing more than I can see.

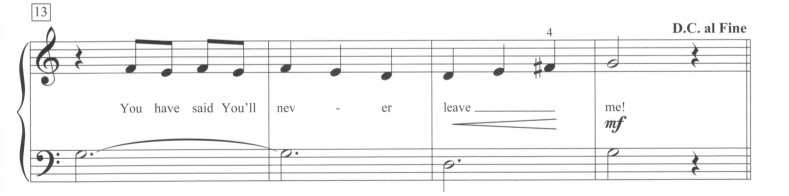

13 You have said You'll nev - er leave _____ me!

D.C. al Fine

mf

"'…I will be with you always, even until the end of this age.'"
– Matthew 28:20, NCV

D.S. al Coda

D.S. al Coda means to go back to the measure marked with the 𝄋 sign, play until the measure marked **To Coda** 𝄌, and skip ahead to the matching Coda sign 𝄌.

Rejoice in the Lord Always
(Based on Philippians 4:4)

Traditional
Arranged by Teresa Ledford

Bring out the L.H. melody!

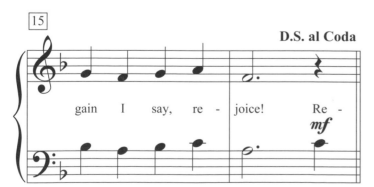 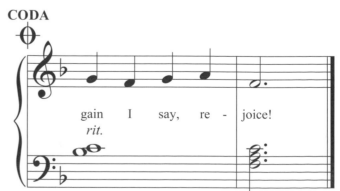

You're playing the prelude at church this Sunday. Follow the instructions above each exercise, and don't be late for the worship service!

- Starting from your house, count the number of measures to the church. _____ How many harmonic 4ths did you pass? _____

- You're picking up a friend who lives 4 measures past the church. How many harmonic 3rds are between the church and your friend's house? _____

- Oh, no! You forgot to bring your music! Go all the way back home to get it (D.C. al Fine). Musicians sometimes call this "going back to the top."

- Now that you have your music, go to the church with your friend (Fine). This time, count the number of harmonic 5ths along the way. _____

- In the next example, count the harmonic 2nds found between the church doors and your Sunday School classroom. _____

- After Sunday School, go 8 measures to the sanctuary entrance. How many harmonic 4ths did you pass?_____

- Oh, no! You left your music behind in the classroom! Go back to the 𝄋 sign and get it (D.S. al Coda). Which measure number is this? _____

- Go 3 measures toward the sanctuary again. Count the number of melodic 3rds you pass. _____

- Uh-oh, the service is about to start! Take the shortcut behind the sanctuary **To Coda** ⊕ directly to the piano at the Coda sign. What is the name of this chord? _____

- Whew! You made it just in time! Turn the page, take a deep breath and play the next piece for the prelude.

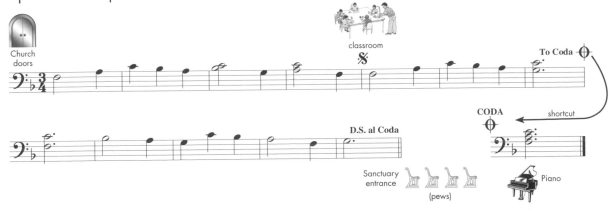

Come, Christians, Join to Sing

Words by Christian Henry Bateman
Traditional Melody
Arranged by Teresa Ledford

Joyfully ♩=112

Bring out the L.H. melody!

Intervals: 6ths

A **6th** is found on a line and a space or a space and a line.
It skips four white keys on the keyboard.

Melodic 6th

Harmonic 6th

🎵 **TRACKS 43-44**

Come Praise His Name

✏️ **Circle all the 6ths in this piece.**

By Wendy Stevens

Happily ♩ = 112

Praise Him in the morn - ing, praise Him in the af - ter - noon,

f

praise Him in the eve - ning. Come praise His name!

2nd time rit.

🎹 **Now, transpose this piece up to the key of F Major.**

🎵 **TRACKS 45-46**

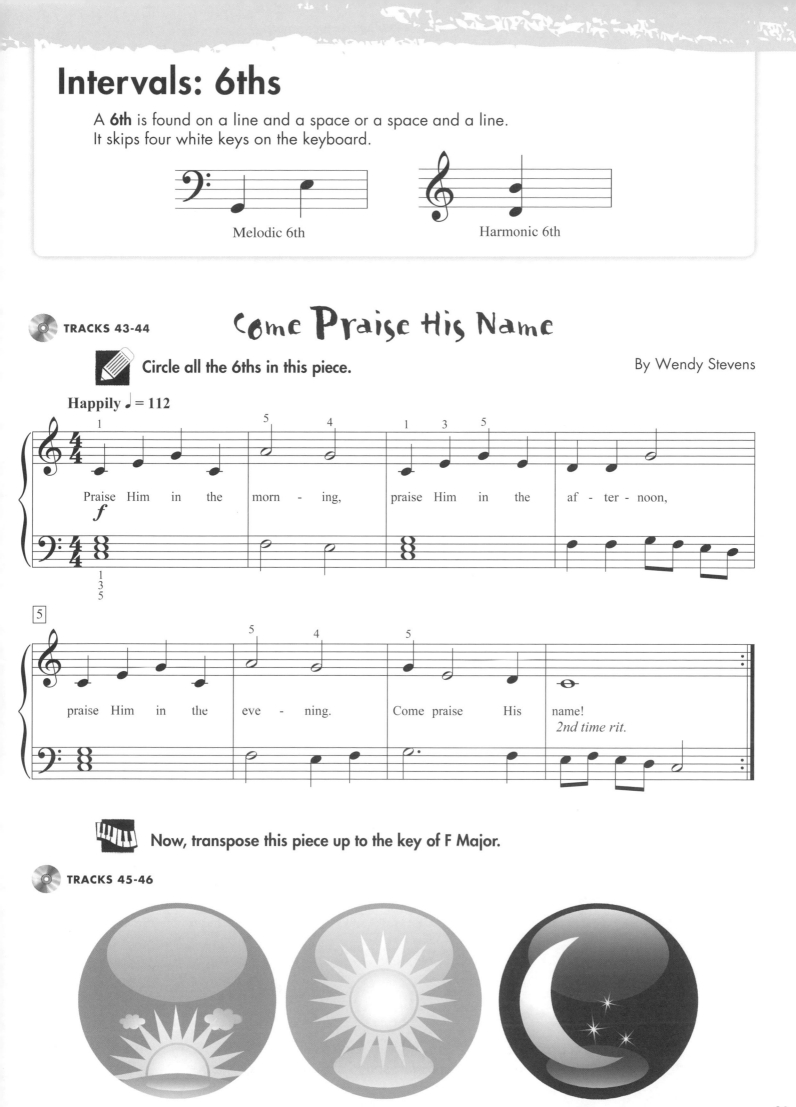

I Want to Sing Praises

Words by Teresa Ledford
Traditional Melody
Arranged by Teresa Ledford

Find and circle the 6ths in this piece.

"Praise the Lord, for the Lord is good;
sing praises to His name, for it is lovely."
– Psalm 135:3, NASB

 Gather a group of people around the piano to sing "I Want to Sing Praises."
Play an intro (the last four measures) and sing this song together.

My Melody of Praise (F Major)

IMPROVISING A MELODY

Improvising is important for any church musician. Some pianists have to improvise during prayers, communion, or other parts of the service. The more you practice improvising, the more comfortable you will become with this skill.

 Improvise your own melody using the six notes below.

- Use steps, skips and repeated notes.
- Use at least one 6th interval.

Improvising Tip: Use a variety of long and short notes in your melody. Let your teacher play the first four measures as an intro to help you feel the $\frac{3}{4}$ meter.

TRACKS 49-50

Gently ♩ = 138

Eighth Note Swing

Eighth notes can be made to sound a little more jazzy if you "swing" them. To swing eighth notes, hold the first one slightly longer than the second one. This will produce an uneven, "long-short" rhythm that's fun to play!

Play this pattern evenly:

Now play it with a swing:

Sing a Joyful Song

TRACKS 51-52

By Wendy Stevens

With a Swing feel ♩ = 112

mf

Sing a lit - tle tune, ____ come and sing a - long.
Sing it mer - ri - ly, ____ tap your toe a - long.

(move L.H. up)

Sing a joy - ful song. ____

(move L.H. down)

Practice this warm-up to work on the finger crossing and the swing feel. Cross finger 2 over your thumb to play the C♯.

Joshua Fit the Battle of Jericho

🎵 **TRACKS 53-54**

Traditional Spiritual
Arranged by Teresa Ledford

Count and clap the R.H. rhythm in measures 2–4 before playing this piece.

New note: D

> "…when the priests blew the trumpets, Joshua said to the people, 'Shout! For the Lord has given you the city.'"
> – Joshua 6:16, NASB

Lead Sheets

COMPING CHORDS

When playing with a group of musicians at church, sometimes the melody is already being played or sung by other members of the group. The pianist must be prepared to "comp" chords when playing with other musicians. "Comp" is short for "accompany." Comping chords can be done a variety of ways.

The easiest way to comp chords is to play the chords with your left hand, which you have already done (see page 10).

If you are not playing the melody, you can comp chords in the right hand instead.

If you play the root of the chord with your left hand and the full chord with your right hand, you will get a better sound.

Keep your left hand in the same place while your right hand moves.

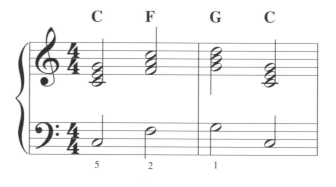

Here is a lead sheet for the first part of "Joyful, Joyful, We Adore Thee." You will learn to comp the chords on the next page.

Words by Henry van Dyke
Music by Ludwig van Beethoven

Joy - ful, joy - ful, we a - dore Thee, God of glo - ry, Lord of love.

Hearts un - fold like flow'rs be - fore Thee, o - p'ning to the sun a - bove.

Joyful, Joyful, We Adore Thee

 Play this lead sheet with your teacher, comping chords as written (chords in the right hand and roots in the left hand).

Words by Henry van Dyke
Music by Ludwig van Beethoven,
melody from *Ninth Symphony*
Adapted by Edward Hodges

TRACKS 55-56

Now try these rhythmic variations for your comping pattern.

Which one do you like best? _____

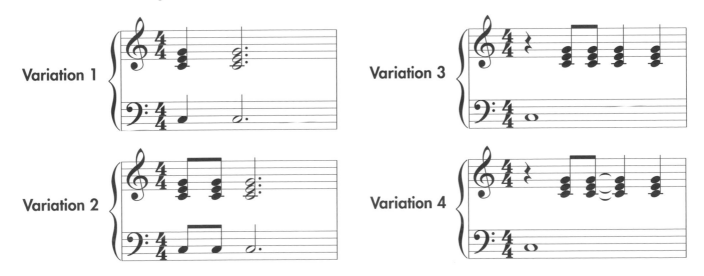

Variation 1

Variation 2

Variation 3

Variation 4

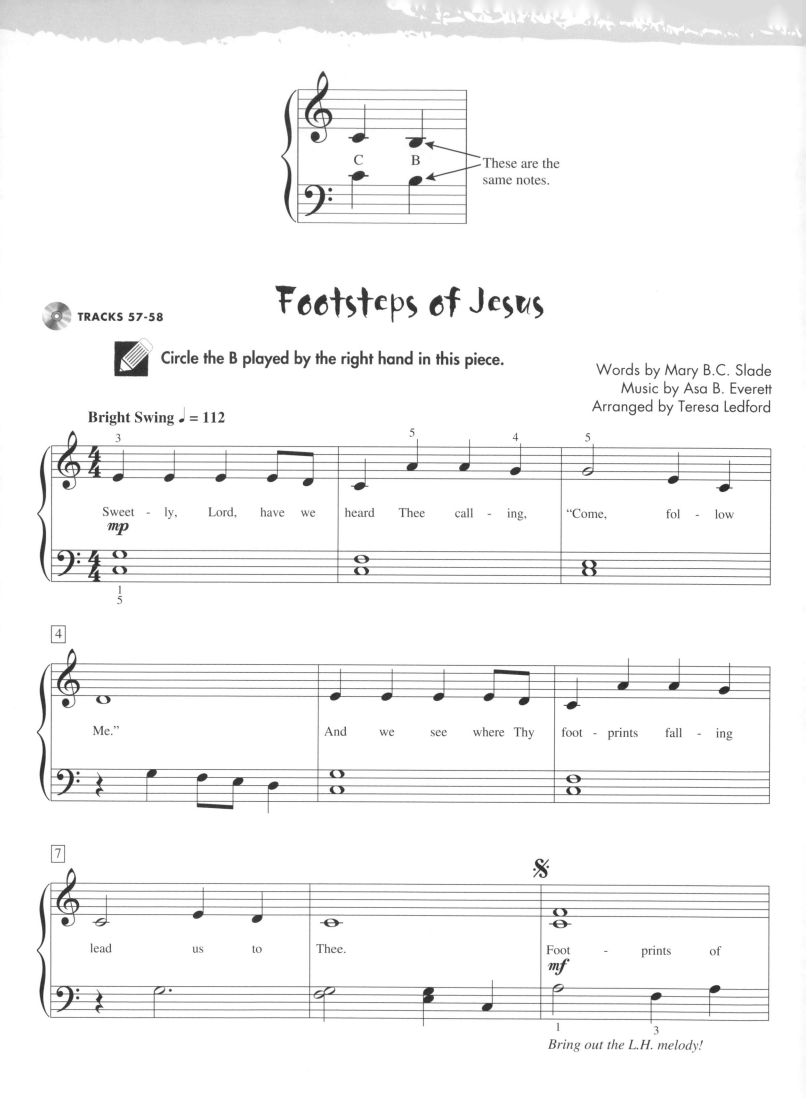

Circle the B played by the right hand in this piece.

Footsteps of Jesus

TRACKS 57-58

Words by Mary B.C. Slade
Music by Asa B. Everett
Arranged by Teresa Ledford

Bright Swing ♩ = 112

Sweet - ly, Lord, have we heard Thee call - ing, "Come, fol - low Me."

And we see where Thy foot - prints fall - ing

lead us to Thee. Foot - prints of

Bring out the L.H. melody!

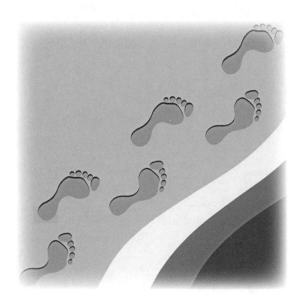

"Jesus said, 'Come follow Me, and I will make you fish for people.'"
– Matthew 4:19, NCV

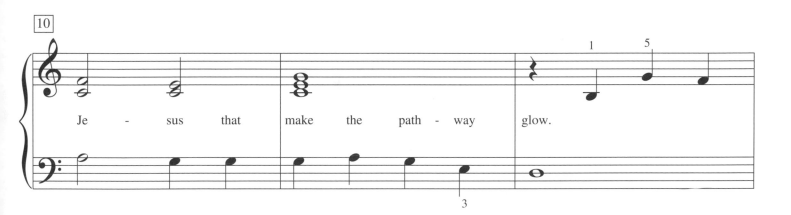

Je - sus that make the path - way glow.

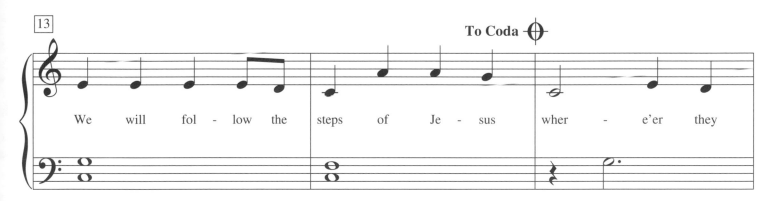

To Coda

We will fol - low the steps of Je - sus wher - e'er they

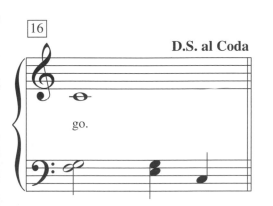

D.S. al Coda

go.

CODA

wher - e'er they go.

41

Dotted Rhythms

Circle the two dotted quarter notes in this piece.

TRACKS 59-60

The B-I-B-L-E

Traditional
Arranged by Teresa Ledford

Brightly ♩ = 120

The B - I - B - L - E, yes, that's the Book for

me. I stand a - lone on the Word of God, the

Bring out the L.H. melody!

B - I - B - L - E! The E!

Play these familiar tunes while counting out loud.

My Jesus, I Love Thee

Words by William R. Featherstone
Music by Adoniram J. Gordon

My Je - sus, I love _____ Thee. I know Thou art mine.

Silent Night, Holy Night

Words by Joseph Mohr
Music by Franz X. Gruber

Si - lent night, ho - ly night.

Softly and Tenderly

Words and Music by
Will L. Thompson

Soft - ly and ten - der - ly, Je - sus is call - ing.

Circle the measures that contain the correct number of beats. Write the counts under the circled measures.

Hear Our Prayer, O Lord

Words based on Psalm 143:1
Music by George Whelpton
Arranged by Teresa Ledford

TRACKS 61-62

Prayerfully ♩ = 92

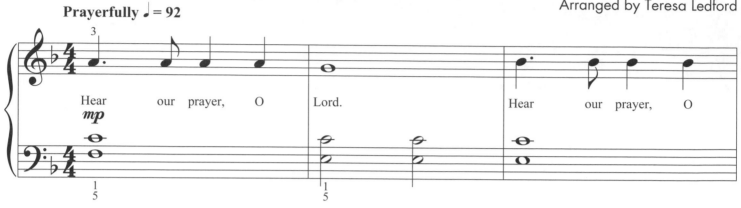

Hear our prayer, O Lord. Hear our prayer, O

Lord. In - cline Thine ear to us, and

*Cross finger 2
over your thumb*

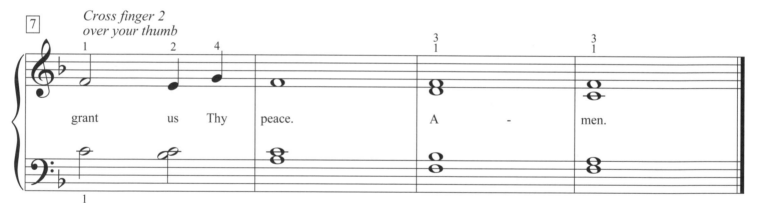

grant us Thy peace. A - men.

 Now, transpose this piece up to the key of G Major.

TRACKS 63-64

*"Lord, hear my prayer; listen to my cry for mercy.
Answer me because You are loyal and good."*

– Psalm 143:1, NCV

Near to the Heart of God

 TRACKS 65-66

Words and Music by
Cleveland McAfee
Altered and Arranged by Teresa Ledford

> "'Take My yoke upon you and learn from Me, for I am gentle and humble in heart, and you will find rest for your souls.'"
>
> – Matthew 11:29, NASB

Play this lead sheet with your teacher, comping chords as written.

TRACKS 67-68

Sweet Hour of Prayer

Words by William W. Walford
Music by William B. Bradbury

Now try these rhythmic variations for your comping pattern.

Which one do you like best? _____

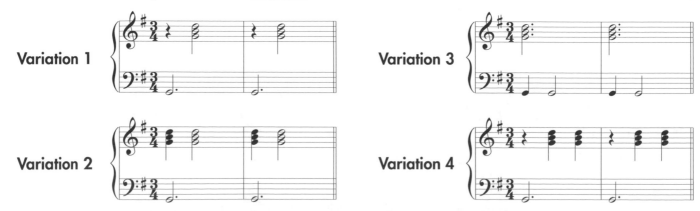

Variation 1

Variation 2

Variation 3

Variation 4

Eighth Rests

Clap and count out loud:

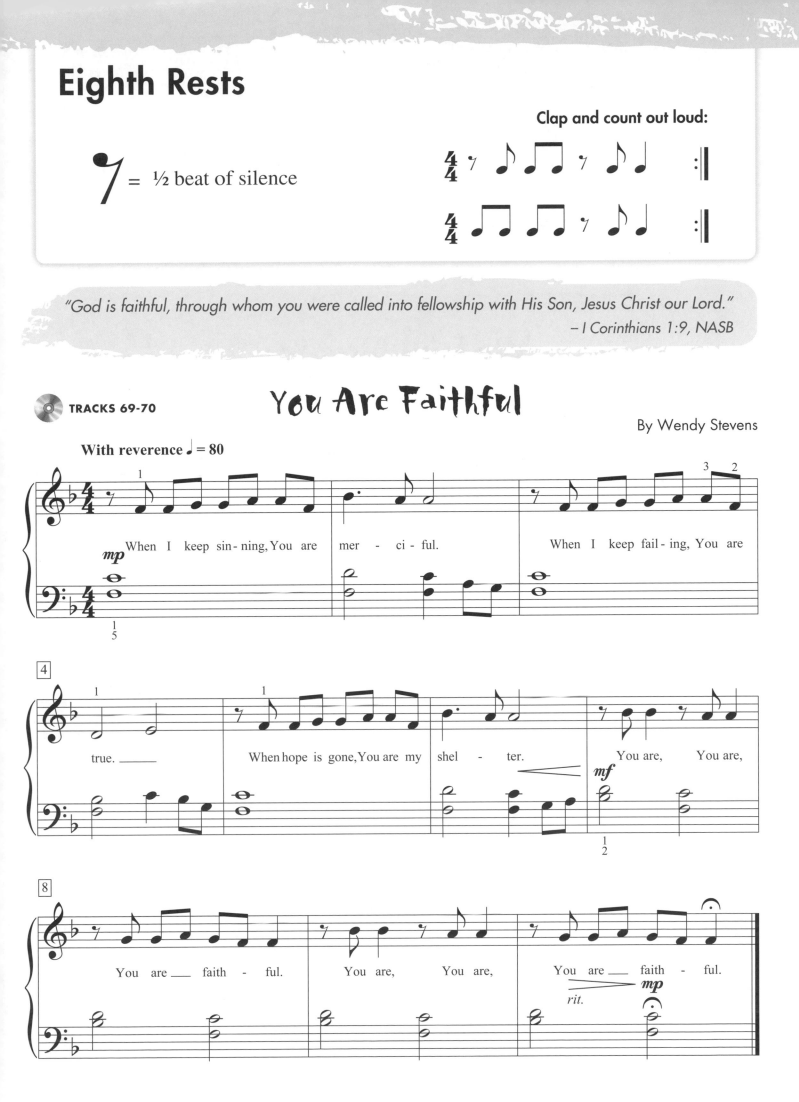

$\dfrac{7}{}$ = ½ beat of silence

"God is faithful, through whom you were called into fellowship with His Son, Jesus Christ our Lord."
– I Corinthians 1:9, NASB

TRACKS 69-70

You Are Faithful

By Wendy Stevens

With reverence ♩ = 80

mp When I keep sin - ning, You are mer - ci - ful. When I keep fail - ing, You are

true. _____ When hope is gone, You are my shel - ter. *mf* You are, You are,

You are ___ faith - ful. You are, You are, You are ___ faith - ful. *rit.* *mp*

47

Syncopation

In the rhythm below, the right-hand quarter note falls on the "&" of beat 1.
This type of "off-beat" rhythm is called syncopation.

Tap this rhythm on your lap while counting out loud:

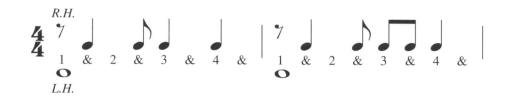

We Will Bless You

TRACKS 71-72

By Wendy Stevens

My Song of Praise (C Major)

Compose your own worship song using these six notes:

1. Draw your melody notes on the treble staff, using the rhythm given.

God   my Fa - ther,   Christ   my King,   Je - sus, Lord of   ev - 'ry - thing;

though You are   so   big   and grand, I   love that You still   hold   my hand.

2. Write an accompaniment on the bass staff, using these intervals to harmonize your melody. Your teacher can help you choose the best sounding harmony and rhythm.

> *"So go and make followers of all people in the world.*
> *Baptize them in the name of the Father and the Son and the Holy Spirit."*
> *— Matthew 28:19, NCV*

Three in One

TRACKS 73-74

By Wendy Stevens

This ancient symbol is sometimes used to represent the Trinity—God the Father, God the Son and God the Holy Spirit. Color the picture to make it your own!

We sing our prais - es to You, give thanks for all that You do.

A - maz - ing, won - der - ful You are to me! God the Fa - ther,

God the Ho - ly Son and God the Spir - it, Three __ in One.

New Note: C

Pedal Technique

The damper pedal is the pedal on the right. To use the damper pedal, place your right heel on the floor with the ball of your foot on the damper pedal. Press the damper pedal down when you see a pedal marking, keeping your heel on the floor.

| Pedal down | Quickly lift and press right after notes are played. | Pedal up |

> **Tip:** Changing the pedal too early will break the sound. Changing the pedal too late will blur the sound.

 Practice this pedaling exercise until it feels natural for you.

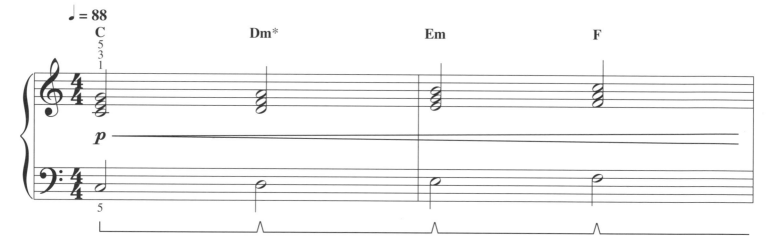

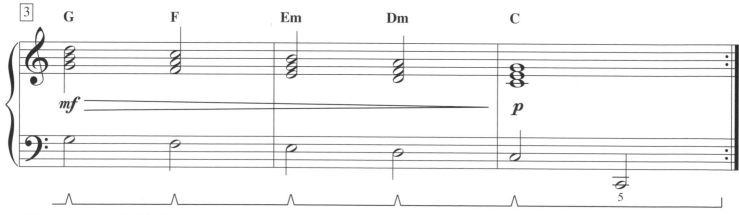

*The lower case "m" indicates that these chords are minor.

Amazing Grace

Words by John Newton
Traditional American Melody
Arranged by Wendy Stevens

TRACKS 75-76

Tip: When using the damper pedal, you can "let go" of notes sooner to move your hand to a new location. For example, try letting go of the D in measure 6 on beat 3 to prepare for the next measure.

TRACKS 77-78

My God

By Teresa Ledford

With confidence ♩ = 104

My God is great and might-y. My God is pure and ho-ly.

There's noth-ing in this world a-bove my God!

My God will al-ways love me. My God will nev-er leave me.

There's noth-ing that can sep-a-rate me from my God!

"Yes, I am sure that neither death, nor life, nor angels, nor ruling spirits, nothing now, nothing in the future, no powers, nothing above us, nothing below us, nor anything else in the whole world will ever be able to separate us from the love of God that is in Christ Jesus our Lord."

– Romans 8:38-39, NCV

54

First Inversion Chords

Inversions are chords whose note order is changed. The name of the chord stays the same, even if the root is not on the bottom.

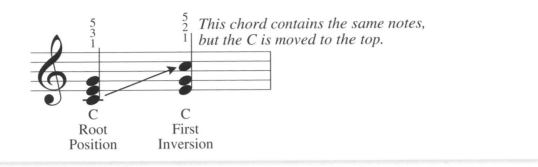

This chord contains the same notes, but the C is moved to the top.

 Practice this pedaling exercise until it feels natural for you.

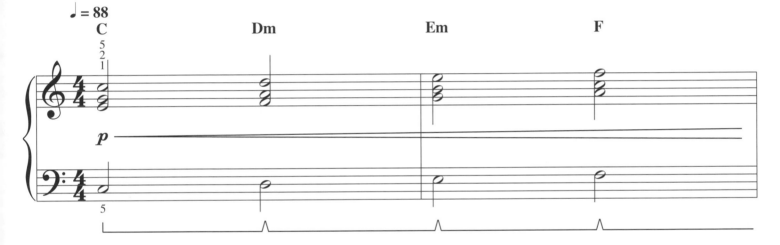

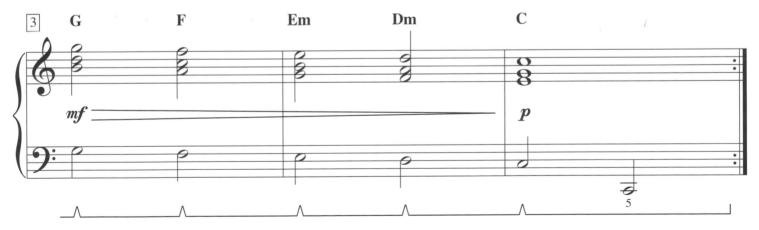

How do these chords compare with the chords on page 52?

_____

_____

Constructing First Inversion Chords

 Name these chords and change them from root position to first inversion.
Remember, the roots of first inversion chords are on top.

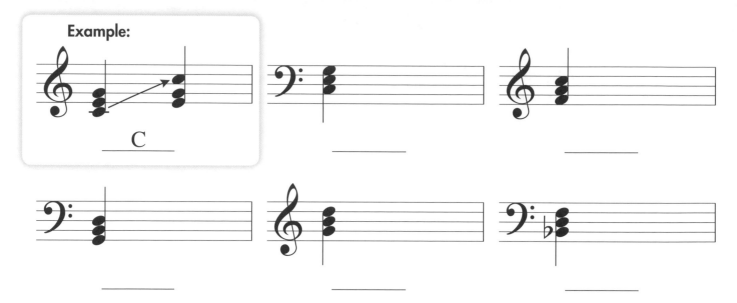

Using First Inversion for Comping

Comping chords will sound even better if you use a few first inversion chords in the right
hand. (This also keeps your right hand from moving around so much!)

 Circle the first inversion chords in this progression.

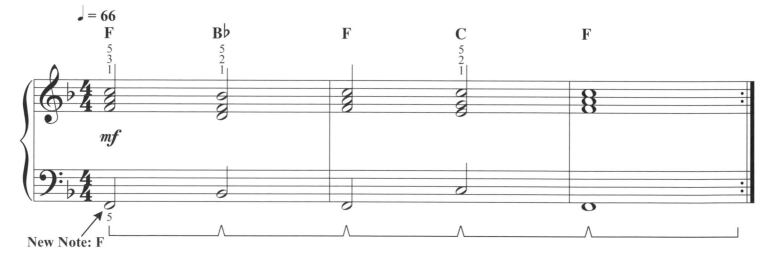

 Practice this progression until you are able to move easily from chord to chord.

Play this lead sheet with your teacher, comping chords as written.

At the Cross

Words by Isaac Watts
and Ralph E. Hudson
Music by Ralph E. Hudson

Now try these rhythmic variations for your comping pattern.

Which one do you like best? _____

Variation 1

Variation 2

Feel free to create your own variations!

In this rhythm exercise, the fourth note is tied over to beat 3. This is another example of **syncopation** (see page 48).

Clap and count out loud:

1   &   2   &   3   &   4   &

The Names of Jesus

TRACKS 81-82

Words by Teresa Ledford
Music by Wendy Stevens

Light of the World, ___ the Bread of Life, ___ Won-der-ful Coun - sel- or, Prince of Peace.

Al-pha, O- me - ga, Lamb of God, ___ Sav-ior, Re-deem - er, Em - man-u - el.

King of kings and Lord of lords, ___ Son of God and Son of Man.

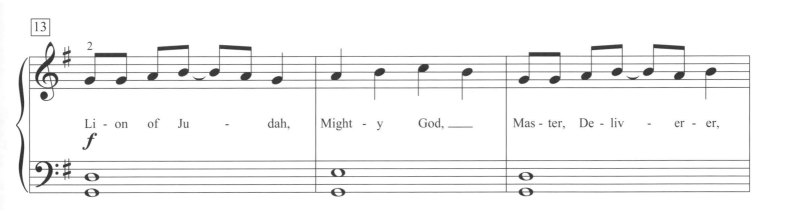

13

Li - on of Ju - dah, Might - y God, ___ Mas - ter, De - liv - er - er,

f

16

Ho - ly One. Shep - herd, Mes - si - ah, Friend of Sin - ners.

19

Name this chord.

He is the Way, ___ He is the Truth, ___ He is the Life. ___ A - men!

Pedal carefully here!

Which name of Jesus means the most to you personally? _____

Write the name of each chord in the blanks below. Remember that the root is not always on the bottom.

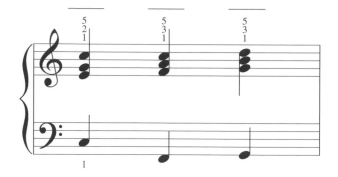

_____   _____   _____

Play this lead sheet with your teacher, comping chords in the above positions.

- Use whole notes the first time, and then try the rhythmic variations on page 57.
- Change the pedal at each barline.
- If no chord is written above a measure, keep playing the previous chord.

When I Survey the Wondrous Cross

TRACKS 83-84

Words by Isaac Watts
Music by Lowell Mason

Reflectively ♩ = 104
(Teacher plays one octave higher.)

Teacher

C   F   C
When I sur - vey the ___ won - drous ___ cross
mp

5
C   F   C   G
on which the Prince of ___ Glo - ry ___ died,

9
C   F   C
my rich - est gain I ___ count but ___ loss,

13
C   F   G   C
and pour con - tempt on all my ___ pride.

✏️ **Write "root" or "first" under each chord.**

F   Bb   C

___ ___ ___

🎹 **Play this lead sheet with your teacher, comping chords in the above positions.**
- Use dotted half notes the first time, and then try the rhythm variations on page 46.
- Change the pedal at each barline.

Praise the Lord! Ye Heavens, Adore Him

TRACKS 85-86

Traditional Words
Music by Rowland H. Prichard

Stately ♩ = 112
(Teacher plays one octave higher.)

Teacher

F

Praise   the   Lord! ____ Ye   heav'ns   a - dore ____ Him.
Sun   and   moon, ____ re - joice   be - fore ____ Him.

Bb   C

5 F

Praise   Him,   an - gels   in ____ the   height.
Praise   Him,   all   ye   stars ____ of   light.

C   F

9 F

Praise   the   Lord, ____ for   He   hath   spo - ken;

Bb   C

13 F

worlds   His   might - y   voice ____ o - beyed.

Bb   C

17 F

Law ____ which   nev - er   shall ____ be   bro - ken,

C   F   C

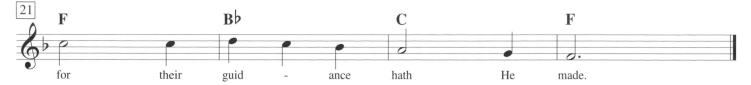

21 F

for   their   guid - ance   hath   He   made.

Bb   C   F

Holy Is the Lord Almighty

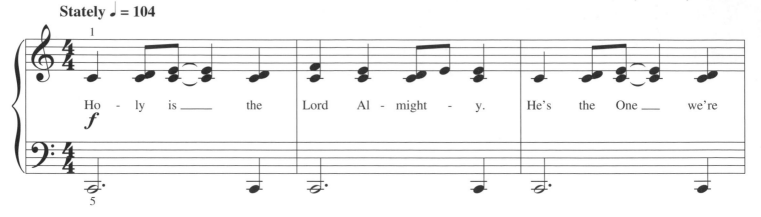

TRACKS 87-88

Words by Teresa Ledford
Music by Wendy Stevens

Stately ♩ = 104

Ho - ly is ___ the Lord Al - might - y. He's the One ___ we're

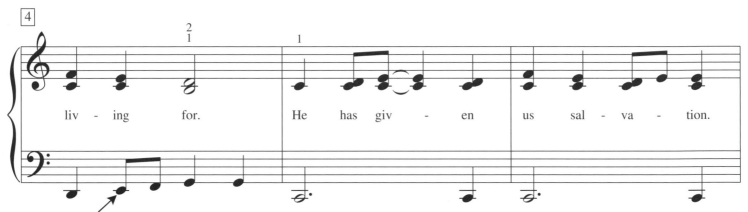

liv - ing for. He has giv - en us sal - va - tion.

New Note: E

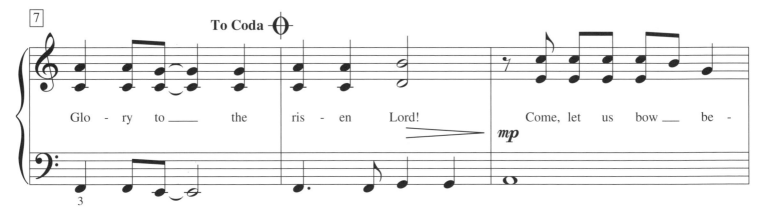

Glo - ry to ___ the ris - en Lord! Come, let us bow ___ be -

"…Holy, Holy, Holy is the Lord of hosts; the whole earth is full of His glory."
– Isaiah 6:3, NASB

fore Him. Come, let us wor - ship and a - dore.

D.C. al Coda

mf He is the King o - ver all the earth, and yet, He loves us more!

CODA

8va

ris - en Lord!

CONGRATULATIONS!

_____

(Student Name)

has completed Level 2 of

the
Worship
PIANO METHOD

Celebrate this achievement by playing your
favorite pieces for your family and friends!

Date _____   Teacher _____